50 Kids in the Kitchen
Recipes for Home

By: Kelly Johnson

Table of Contents

- Mini Pizzas
- Fruit Kabobs
- Veggie Wraps
- Pancake Faces
- Cheesy Quesadillas
- DIY Trail Mix
- Banana Sushi
- Rainbow Smoothies
- Apple Sandwiches
- Homemade Chicken Nuggets
- Rice Krispie Treats
- Pita Pocket Sandwiches
- Spaghetti Nests
- Ants on a Log
- No-Bake Energy Bites
- Muffin Tin Omelets
- Yogurt Parfaits
- Chocolate-Dipped Pretzels
- Mini Tacos
- Cucumber Sandwiches
- Easy Fruit Salad
- Egg-in-a-Hole
- Sliders
- Homemade Popcorn
- Pizza Bagels
- Frozen Yogurt Bark
- Cheesy Broccoli Bites
- Veggie Faces on Toast
- Simple Smoothie Bowls
- Pancake Muffins
- Sweet Potato Fries
- Cookie Decorating
- Fruit and Yogurt Popsicles
- Mini Meatloaf
- Grilled Cheese Roll-Ups

- Cauliflower Pizza Crust
- Homemade Guacamole
- Peanut Butter Banana Bites
- Savory Scones
- S'mores Dip
- Fruit and Cheese Skewers
- Veggie Noodle Stir-Fry
- Chocolate Chip Cookies
- Cheesy Cauliflower Tots
- Simple Sushi Rolls
- Egg Salad Sandwiches
- Rainbow Veggie Pizza
- Mac and Cheese Cups
- Oatmeal Cookies
- Fruit Smoothie Pops

Mini Pizzas

Ingredients:

For the Base:

- 1 package (about 8 oz) of pre-made pizza dough or biscuit dough
- 1/2 cup pizza sauce (store-bought or homemade)

Toppings:

- 1 cup shredded mozzarella cheese
- Pepperoni slices (or any toppings you prefer: bell peppers, olives, mushrooms, etc.)
- 1 tsp dried oregano or Italian seasoning
- Fresh basil leaves (optional, for garnish)

Instructions:

1. **Preheat the Oven:** Preheat your oven to 400°F (200°C).
2. **Prepare the Dough:** Roll out the pizza dough on a floured surface to about 1/4 inch thick. If using biscuit dough, separate it into individual biscuits and flatten each one.
3. **Cut Out the Bases:** Use a cookie cutter or a cup to cut out small rounds from the dough (about 3-4 inches in diameter). Place them on a baking sheet lined with parchment paper.
4. **Add Sauce:** Spoon a small amount of pizza sauce onto each dough round, spreading it slightly, leaving a little edge.
5. **Add Toppings:** Sprinkle shredded mozzarella cheese on top of the sauce. Add your desired toppings and a sprinkle of oregano.
6. **Bake:** Bake in the preheated oven for about 10-12 minutes, or until the cheese is bubbly and the edges are golden.
7. **Serve:** Remove from the oven and let cool slightly. Garnish with fresh basil if desired. Serve warm!

Tips:

- Customize your mini pizzas with different sauces (like pesto or alfredo) or cheeses.
- Great for parties; let guests assemble their own with a toppings bar!

Enjoy your mini pizzas!

Fruit Kabobs

Ingredients:

- Assorted fruits (e.g., strawberries, grapes, pineapple, melon, banana)
- Wooden skewers
- Optional: yogurt or chocolate for dipping

Instructions:

1. **Prepare the Fruit:** Wash and cut the fruits into bite-sized pieces.
2. **Assemble the Kabobs:** Thread the fruit pieces onto the wooden skewers, alternating colors and types for a vibrant look.
3. **Serve:** Arrange the kabobs on a platter. If desired, serve with yogurt or melted chocolate for dipping.

Veggie Wraps

Ingredients:

- 4 large tortillas (whole wheat or flour)
- 1 cup hummus or cream cheese
- 1 cup assorted veggies (e.g., bell peppers, carrots, cucumber, spinach, avocado)
- Optional: sliced turkey or chicken, cheese

Instructions:

1. **Spread the Base:** Spread a generous layer of hummus or cream cheese over each tortilla.
2. **Add Veggies:** Layer the assorted veggies and any optional ingredients evenly on top.
3. **Roll the Wrap:** Tightly roll each tortilla from one end to the other. Slice into pinwheels or halves.
4. **Serve:** Arrange on a plate and enjoy as a healthy snack or lunch!

Pancake Faces

Ingredients:

- 1 cup pancake mix
- Water or milk (as directed on pancake mix)
- Assorted toppings (e.g., sliced bananas, blueberries, chocolate chips, whipped cream)

Instructions:

1. **Make the Pancakes:** Prepare the pancake batter according to the package instructions.
2. **Cook the Pancakes:** Heat a skillet over medium heat and pour batter to form small pancakes (about 4-6 inches in diameter). Cook until bubbles form, then flip and cook until golden brown.
3. **Create Faces:** Once cooked, use the toppings to create fun faces on each pancake. Use banana slices for eyes, blueberries for pupils, and chocolate chips for smiles.
4. **Serve:** Serve immediately with syrup or additional toppings on the side.

Enjoy these fun recipes with friends and family!

Cheesy Quesadillas

Ingredients:

- 4 flour tortillas
- 2 cups shredded cheese (cheddar, mozzarella, or a mix)
- Optional: cooked chicken, black beans, or veggies (like bell peppers)
- Salsa or sour cream for serving

Instructions:

1. **Assemble Quesadillas:** Place one tortilla in a skillet over medium heat. Sprinkle half with cheese and any optional fillings. Fold the other half over.
2. **Cook:** Cook for about 2-3 minutes on each side until golden and the cheese is melted.
3. **Serve:** Cut into wedges and serve with salsa or sour cream.

DIY Trail Mix

Ingredients:

- 1 cup nuts (almonds, cashews, peanuts)
- 1 cup dried fruit (raisins, cranberries, apricots)
- 1 cup seeds (pumpkin seeds, sunflower seeds)
- 1 cup chocolate chips or yogurt-covered snacks (optional)

Instructions:

1. **Mix Ingredients:** In a large bowl, combine all the ingredients.
2. **Store:** Portion into snack bags or containers for easy grab-and-go snacks.

Banana Sushi

Ingredients:

- 2 bananas
- 2 tbsp nut butter (peanut, almond, or sunflower)
- Optional toppings: granola, shredded coconut, mini chocolate chips

Instructions:

1. **Spread Nut Butter:** Spread nut butter evenly over each banana.
2. **Add Toppings:** Roll the banana in granola or your choice of toppings.
3. **Slice:** Slice into bite-sized pieces and enjoy!

Rainbow Smoothies

Ingredients:

- 1 cup spinach or kale (for green layer)
- 1 cup frozen mixed berries (for red/purple layer)
- 1 cup mango or pineapple (for yellow/orange layer)
- 1 cup banana or yogurt (for white layer)
- Optional: honey or agave syrup for sweetness

Instructions:

1. **Blend Layers:** Blend each fruit/vegetable layer separately until smooth.
2. **Layer in Glass:** Pour each layer into a clear glass, starting with the purple, then yellow, green, and white.
3. **Serve:** Enjoy immediately with a straw!

Apple Sandwiches

Ingredients:

- 2 apples
- 2-4 tbsp nut butter
- Optional: granola, raisins, or chocolate chips

Instructions:

1. **Slice Apples:** Core and slice apples into thick rounds.
2. **Spread Nut Butter:** Spread nut butter on one apple slice, top with granola or other toppings, and then place another slice on top to make a sandwich.
3. **Serve:** Enjoy as a fun and healthy snack!

Homemade Chicken Nuggets

Ingredients:

- 1 lb chicken breast, cut into bite-sized pieces
- 1 cup breadcrumbs (Panko works well)
- 1/2 cup flour
- 1 egg, beaten
- Optional: spices (garlic powder, paprika, salt)

Instructions:

1. **Preheat Oven:** Preheat oven to 400°F (200°C).
2. **Coat Chicken:** Dredge chicken pieces in flour, dip in egg, and then coat with breadcrumbs.
3. **Bake:** Place on a baking sheet and bake for 15-20 minutes, until golden and cooked through.
4. **Serve:** Serve with your favorite dipping sauce.

Rice Krispie Treats

Ingredients:

- 3 tbsp butter
- 1 package (10 oz) marshmallows (or 4 cups mini marshmallows)
- 6 cups Rice Krispies cereal

Instructions:

1. **Melt Butter and Marshmallows:** In a large pot, melt butter over low heat. Add marshmallows and stir until completely melted.
2. **Mix in Cereal:** Remove from heat and add Rice Krispies, stirring until well coated.
3. **Shape Treats:** Press the mixture into a greased 9x13 inch pan and let cool. Cut into squares.

Pita Pocket Sandwiches

Ingredients:

- 4 whole wheat pita pockets
- 1 cup hummus or tzatziki
- 1 cup assorted veggies (cucumber, lettuce, tomatoes, bell peppers)
- Optional: sliced turkey, chicken, or cheese

Instructions:

1. **Prepare Pita:** Cut the pita pockets in half to create pockets.
2. **Fill Pockets:** Spread hummus inside each pocket and fill with veggies and optional protein.
3. **Serve:** Enjoy as a healthy and portable meal!

Enjoy making and sharing these delicious recipes!

Spaghetti Nests

Ingredients:

- 8 oz spaghetti
- 2 eggs
- 1 cup shredded mozzarella cheese
- Salt and pepper to taste
- Marinara sauce (for serving)

Instructions:

1. **Cook Spaghetti:** Cook spaghetti according to package instructions; drain and let cool slightly.
2. **Mix Ingredients:** In a bowl, mix cooked spaghetti, eggs, cheese, salt, and pepper.
3. **Form Nests:** Preheat the oven to 375°F (190°C). Grease a muffin tin and twirl spaghetti mixture into each cup, forming nests.
4. **Bake:** Bake for 15-20 minutes until golden. Serve with marinara sauce.

Ants on a Log

Ingredients:

- 4 celery sticks
- 1/2 cup peanut butter or nut butter
- 1/2 cup raisins or chocolate chips

Instructions:

1. **Prepare Celery:** Wash and cut celery sticks into 3-4 inch pieces.
2. **Spread Nut Butter:** Spread peanut butter into the grooves of the celery sticks.
3. **Add "Ants":** Top with raisins or chocolate chips to create "ants." Serve as a fun snack!

No-Bake Energy Bites

Ingredients:

- 1 cup rolled oats
- 1/2 cup nut butter (peanut, almond, etc.)
- 1/3 cup honey or maple syrup
- 1/2 cup chocolate chips
- 1/4 cup chia seeds or flax seeds (optional)

Instructions:

1. **Mix Ingredients:** In a bowl, combine all ingredients and mix well.
2. **Form Bites:** Roll the mixture into small balls (about 1 inch).
3. **Chill:** Refrigerate for at least 30 minutes to firm up. Enjoy as a quick snack!

Muffin Tin Omelets

Ingredients:

- 6 large eggs
- 1/4 cup milk
- 1 cup diced veggies (bell peppers, spinach, tomatoes)
- 1 cup shredded cheese
- Salt and pepper to taste

Instructions:

1. **Preheat Oven:** Preheat the oven to 350°F (175°C) and grease a muffin tin.
2. **Mix Eggs:** In a bowl, whisk together eggs, milk, salt, and pepper.
3. **Fill Muffin Tin:** Divide veggies and cheese among muffin cups, then pour the egg mixture over the top.
4. **Bake:** Bake for 20-25 minutes until set. Let cool slightly before removing.

Yogurt Parfaits

Ingredients:

- 2 cups yogurt (plain or flavored)
- 1 cup granola
- 2 cups mixed berries (strawberries, blueberries, raspberries)

Instructions:

1. **Layer Ingredients:** In cups or bowls, layer yogurt, granola, and berries.
2. **Repeat Layers:** Continue layering until ingredients are used up.
3. **Serve:** Enjoy immediately for a refreshing snack or breakfast!

Chocolate-Dipped Pretzels

Ingredients:

- 2 cups pretzel rods or twists
- 1 cup chocolate chips (milk, dark, or white chocolate)
- Optional: sprinkles or crushed nuts for topping

Instructions:

1. **Melt Chocolate:** Melt chocolate chips in a microwave-safe bowl in 30-second increments, stirring until smooth.
2. **Dip Pretzels:** Dip each pretzel into the melted chocolate, letting excess drip off.
3. **Decorate:** Place on parchment paper and sprinkle with toppings if desired.
4. **Cool:** Let cool until chocolate hardens.

Mini Tacos

Ingredients:

- 1 lb ground beef or turkey
- 1 packet taco seasoning
- 12 mini flour or corn tortillas
- Toppings: shredded cheese, lettuce, diced tomatoes, salsa

Instructions:

1. **Cook Meat:** In a skillet, cook ground meat until browned. Add taco seasoning and water according to package instructions.
2. **Assemble Tacos:** Fill mini tortillas with meat and desired toppings.
3. **Serve:** Enjoy as a fun meal or snack!

Cucumber Sandwiches

Ingredients:

- 1 large cucumber
- 1 cup cream cheese (plain or flavored)
- 8 slices of bread (white, whole grain, or rye)
- Optional: fresh herbs (dill or chives)

Instructions:

1. **Slice Cucumber:** Thinly slice the cucumber.
2. **Spread Cream Cheese:** Spread cream cheese on one side of each slice of bread.
3. **Layer:** Top half the bread slices with cucumber slices and herbs, then place the other half on top.
4. **Cut and Serve:** Cut into quarters or triangles and serve as a refreshing snack!

Enjoy making these tasty treats!

Easy Fruit Salad

Ingredients:

- 2 cups strawberries, hulled and sliced
- 1 cup blueberries
- 1 cup pineapple, diced
- 1 cup grapes, halved
- 1 banana, sliced
- Optional: 1 tbsp honey or lime juice

Instructions:

1. **Combine Fruit:** In a large bowl, combine all the fruits.
2. **Add Sweetener:** If desired, drizzle with honey or lime juice and gently toss to combine.
3. **Serve:** Enjoy immediately or chill in the refrigerator for 30 minutes.

Egg-in-a-Hole

Ingredients:

- 2 slices of bread
- 2 eggs
- Butter or oil for cooking
- Salt and pepper to taste

Instructions:

1. **Cut Bread:** Use a cookie cutter or glass to cut a hole in the center of each bread slice.
2. **Cook:** Heat butter or oil in a skillet over medium heat. Place the bread in the skillet and crack an egg into each hole.
3. **Season:** Sprinkle with salt and pepper. Cook until the egg is set to your liking, about 3-5 minutes.
4. **Serve:** Enjoy warm!

Sliders

Ingredients:

- 1 lb ground beef or turkey
- 1 packet seasoning (like ranch or taco)
- 12 slider buns
- Cheese slices (optional)
- Toppings: lettuce, tomato, pickles, ketchup, mustard

Instructions:

1. **Cook Meat:** In a skillet, cook the ground meat with the seasoning until browned.
2. **Form Sliders:** Shape the meat into small patties (about 2-3 inches wide).
3. **Cook Patties:** Cook in the skillet for about 3-4 minutes per side. Add cheese slices on top during the last minute if using.
4. **Assemble:** Place patties on slider buns with desired toppings and serve.

Homemade Popcorn

Ingredients:

- 1/2 cup popcorn kernels
- 2-3 tbsp vegetable oil or coconut oil
- Salt to taste

Instructions:

1. **Heat Oil:** In a large pot, heat oil over medium heat.
2. **Add Kernels:** Add popcorn kernels and cover the pot.
3. **Pop:** Shake the pot occasionally until popping slows down. Remove from heat.
4. **Season:** Sprinkle with salt and toss to coat. Serve warm!

Pizza Bagels

Ingredients:

- 4 bagel halves
- 1/2 cup pizza sauce
- 1 cup shredded mozzarella cheese
- Toppings: pepperoni, olives, veggies, etc.

Instructions:

1. **Preheat Oven:** Preheat the oven to 375°F (190°C).
2. **Assemble:** Spread pizza sauce on each bagel half. Top with cheese and desired toppings.
3. **Bake:** Place on a baking sheet and bake for 10-12 minutes, until cheese is melted.
4. **Serve:** Enjoy warm!

Frozen Yogurt Bark

Ingredients:

- 2 cups yogurt (any flavor)
- 1/2 cup mixed berries (strawberries, blueberries, raspberries)
- 1/4 cup granola or nuts (optional)

Instructions:

1. **Spread Yogurt:** Line a baking sheet with parchment paper. Spread yogurt evenly over the sheet.
2. **Add Toppings:** Sprinkle berries and granola on top.
3. **Freeze:** Freeze for at least 3 hours until firm.
4. **Break and Serve:** Break into pieces and enjoy as a cool snack!

Cheesy Broccoli Bites

Ingredients:

- 2 cups steamed broccoli, chopped
- 1 cup shredded cheese (cheddar or mozzarella)
- 1/2 cup breadcrumbs
- 1 egg
- Salt and pepper to taste

Instructions:

1. **Preheat Oven:** Preheat the oven to 375°F (190°C) and grease a baking sheet.
2. **Mix Ingredients:** In a bowl, combine chopped broccoli, cheese, breadcrumbs, egg, salt, and pepper.
3. **Form Bites:** Shape into small balls and place on the baking sheet.
4. **Bake:** Bake for 15-20 minutes until golden. Serve warm!

Veggie Faces on Toast

Ingredients:

- 4 slices of bread (whole grain or white)
- 1/2 cup cream cheese or hummus
- Assorted veggies (cucumber slices, bell pepper strips, cherry tomatoes, olives)

Instructions:

1. **Spread Base:** Toast bread slices and spread cream cheese or hummus on top.
2. **Create Faces:** Use assorted veggies to create fun faces on each slice.
3. **Serve:** Cut into halves or quarters and enjoy!

Simple Smoothie Bowls

Ingredients:

- 1 cup frozen fruit (banana, berries, mango)
- 1/2 cup yogurt or milk
- Toppings: granola, fresh fruit, nuts, seeds

Instructions:

1. **Blend Base:** In a blender, combine frozen fruit and yogurt/milk until smooth.
2. **Pour into Bowls:** Pour the smoothie into bowls.
3. **Add Toppings:** Top with granola, fresh fruit, and nuts. Enjoy with a spoon!

Enjoy making and sharing these delicious recipes!

Pancake Muffins

Ingredients:

- 1 cup pancake mix
- 1 cup milk
- 1 egg
- 1/2 cup chocolate chips or blueberries (optional)

Instructions:

1. **Preheat Oven:** Preheat the oven to 350°F (175°C) and grease a muffin tin.
2. **Mix Ingredients:** In a bowl, combine pancake mix, milk, and egg until just mixed. Fold in chocolate chips or blueberries if using.
3. **Fill Muffin Tin:** Pour the batter into the muffin tin, filling each cup about 2/3 full.
4. **Bake:** Bake for 15-20 minutes, or until a toothpick inserted comes out clean. Let cool slightly before serving.

Sweet Potato Fries

Ingredients:

- 2 large sweet potatoes
- 2 tbsp olive oil
- 1 tsp paprika
- Salt and pepper to taste

Instructions:

1. **Preheat Oven:** Preheat the oven to 425°F (220°C).
2. **Cut Sweet Potatoes:** Peel and cut sweet potatoes into thin wedges.
3. **Season:** Toss the wedges with olive oil, paprika, salt, and pepper.
4. **Bake:** Spread on a baking sheet in a single layer and bake for 25-30 minutes, flipping halfway through, until crispy.

Cookie Decorating

Ingredients:

- 1 batch of sugar cookies (store-bought or homemade)
- Royal icing or frosting (store-bought or homemade)
- Assorted toppings: sprinkles, edible glitter, chocolate chips, etc.

Instructions:

1. **Bake Cookies:** Bake sugar cookies according to recipe or package instructions and let cool completely.
2. **Prepare Icing:** If using royal icing, prepare according to instructions.
3. **Decorate:** Use icing to decorate the cookies and add toppings as desired. Let the cookies set before serving.

Fruit and Yogurt Popsicles

Ingredients:

- 2 cups yogurt (any flavor)
- 2 cups mixed fruit (berries, bananas, mango)
- Optional: honey or maple syrup for sweetness

Instructions:

1. **Layer Ingredients:** In popsicle molds, layer yogurt and fruit.
2. **Blend (Optional):** For a smoother texture, blend the yogurt and fruit together before pouring into molds.
3. **Freeze:** Insert sticks and freeze for at least 4 hours until solid.
4. **Serve:** Run warm water over the outside of the molds to help release the popsicles.

Mini Meatloaf

Ingredients:

- 1 lb ground beef or turkey
- 1/2 cup breadcrumbs
- 1/4 cup ketchup
- 1 egg
- Salt and pepper to taste
- Optional: diced onions or bell peppers

Instructions:

1. **Preheat Oven:** Preheat the oven to 350°F (175°C) and grease a muffin tin.
2. **Mix Ingredients:** In a bowl, combine ground meat, breadcrumbs, ketchup, egg, salt, and pepper (and any optional veggies).
3. **Shape Meatloaf:** Divide the mixture among the muffin tin cups, pressing down slightly.
4. **Bake:** Bake for 20-25 minutes until cooked through. Serve warm!

Grilled Cheese Roll-Ups

Ingredients:

- 4 slices of bread
- 4 slices of cheese (cheddar, mozzarella, etc.)
- Butter for cooking

Instructions:

1. **Flatten Bread:** Use a rolling pin to flatten each slice of bread.
2. **Assemble:** Place a slice of cheese on each piece of bread and roll them up tightly.
3. **Cook:** Heat a skillet over medium heat and melt some butter. Place the roll-ups seam side down and cook until golden on all sides.
4. **Serve:** Cut in half and enjoy warm!

Cauliflower Pizza Crust

Ingredients:

- 1 medium cauliflower, grated (about 2-3 cups)
- 1/2 cup shredded mozzarella cheese
- 1/4 cup grated Parmesan cheese
- 1 egg
- 1 tsp dried oregano
- Salt and pepper to taste

Instructions:

1. **Preheat Oven:** Preheat the oven to 425°F (220°C) and line a baking sheet with parchment paper.
2. **Prepare Cauliflower:** Steam and then let the grated cauliflower cool. Squeeze out excess moisture using a clean kitchen towel.
3. **Mix Ingredients:** In a bowl, combine cauliflower, mozzarella, Parmesan, egg, oregano, salt, and pepper.
4. **Shape Crust:** Spread the mixture onto the baking sheet in a round shape, about 1/4 inch thick.
5. **Bake:** Bake for 15-20 minutes until golden. Add toppings and bake again for another 10 minutes.

Homemade Guacamole

Ingredients:

- 2 ripe avocados
- 1 small onion, diced
- 1 tomato, diced
- 1 lime, juiced
- Salt and pepper to taste
- Optional: chopped cilantro or jalapeño

Instructions:

1. **Mash Avocados:** In a bowl, mash the avocados with a fork.
2. **Add Ingredients:** Stir in onion, tomato, lime juice, salt, and pepper (and any optional ingredients).
3. **Serve:** Enjoy with tortilla chips or as a topping for tacos!

Peanut Butter Banana Bites

Ingredients:

- 2 bananas
- 1/2 cup peanut butter
- 1/4 cup granola or crushed nuts (optional)

Instructions:

1. **Slice Bananas:** Slice bananas into 1/2-inch rounds.
2. **Spread Peanut Butter:** Spread peanut butter on half of the banana slices and top with the other half to make sandwiches.
3. **Coat (Optional):** Roll the edges in granola or crushed nuts if desired.
4. **Serve:** Enjoy as a quick snack!

Enjoy making and sharing these tasty recipes!

Savory Scones

Ingredients:

- 2 cups all-purpose flour
- 1 tbsp baking powder
- 1/2 tsp salt
- 1/2 cup cold butter, cubed
- 1 cup shredded cheese (cheddar, feta, or your choice)
- 1/2 cup chopped herbs (chives, parsley, or spinach)
- 3/4 cup milk

Instructions:

1. **Preheat Oven:** Preheat the oven to 400°F (200°C) and line a baking sheet with parchment paper.
2. **Mix Dry Ingredients:** In a bowl, combine flour, baking powder, and salt.
3. **Cut in Butter:** Add cold butter and mix until the mixture resembles coarse crumbs.
4. **Add Cheese and Herbs:** Stir in cheese and herbs.
5. **Add Milk:** Pour in milk and mix until just combined.
6. **Shape and Bake:** Turn the dough onto a floured surface, shape into a circle, and cut into wedges. Place on the baking sheet and bake for 15-20 minutes until golden.

S'mores Dip

Ingredients:

- 1 cup chocolate chips (milk or dark)
- 1 cup mini marshmallows
- Graham crackers for dipping

Instructions:

1. **Preheat Oven:** Preheat the oven to 450°F (230°C).
2. **Layer Ingredients:** In an oven-safe dish, layer chocolate chips and top with mini marshmallows.
3. **Bake:** Bake for 5-7 minutes until the marshmallows are golden and the chocolate is melted.
4. **Serve:** Serve warm with graham crackers for dipping.

Fruit and Cheese Skewers

Ingredients:

- Assorted fruits (grapes, strawberries, melon, pineapple)
- Assorted cheeses (cheddar, mozzarella, gouda)
- Wooden skewers

Instructions:

1. **Prepare Ingredients:** Cut fruits and cheese into bite-sized pieces.
2. **Assemble Skewers:** Alternate threading pieces of fruit and cheese onto the skewers.
3. **Serve:** Arrange on a platter and enjoy as a refreshing snack!

Veggie Noodle Stir-Fry

Ingredients:

- 2 cups vegetable noodles (zucchini, carrot, or any vegetable)
- 1 cup mixed veggies (bell peppers, broccoli, snap peas)
- 2 tbsp soy sauce
- 1 tbsp olive oil
- 1 tsp garlic, minced
- Optional: sesame seeds for garnish

Instructions:

1. **Heat Oil:** In a large skillet, heat olive oil over medium heat.
2. **Add Garlic:** Add minced garlic and sauté for about 30 seconds.
3. **Stir-Fry Veggies:** Add mixed veggies and stir-fry for 3-4 minutes.
4. **Add Noodles:** Stir in veggie noodles and soy sauce, cooking for an additional 3-5 minutes until tender.
5. **Serve:** Garnish with sesame seeds if desired and enjoy!

Chocolate Chip Cookies

Ingredients:

- 1 cup butter, softened
- 3/4 cup brown sugar
- 3/4 cup granulated sugar
- 1 tsp vanilla extract
- 2 eggs
- 2 1/4 cups all-purpose flour
- 1 tsp baking soda
- 1/2 tsp salt
- 2 cups chocolate chips

Instructions:

1. **Preheat Oven:** Preheat the oven to 350°F (175°C) and line a baking sheet with parchment paper.
2. **Cream Butter and Sugars:** In a large bowl, cream together butter, brown sugar, and granulated sugar until light and fluffy.
3. **Add Eggs and Vanilla:** Beat in eggs one at a time, then stir in vanilla.
4. **Mix Dry Ingredients:** In another bowl, whisk together flour, baking soda, and salt. Gradually add to the butter mixture.
5. **Fold in Chocolate Chips:** Stir in chocolate chips.
6. **Drop Cookies:** Drop rounded tablespoons of dough onto the baking sheet.
7. **Bake:** Bake for 10-12 minutes, or until golden around the edges. Let cool on a wire rack.

Cheesy Cauliflower Tots

Ingredients:

- 1 small head cauliflower, grated
- 1 cup shredded cheese (cheddar or mozzarella)
- 1/2 cup breadcrumbs
- 1 egg
- 1 tsp garlic powder
- Salt and pepper to taste

Instructions:

1. **Preheat Oven:** Preheat the oven to 400°F (200°C) and line a baking sheet with parchment paper.
2. **Steam Cauliflower:** Steam and then let the grated cauliflower cool. Squeeze out excess moisture using a clean kitchen towel.
3. **Mix Ingredients:** In a bowl, combine cauliflower, cheese, breadcrumbs, egg, garlic powder, salt, and pepper.
4. **Form Tots:** Shape the mixture into small tots and place them on the baking sheet.
5. **Bake:** Bake for 20-25 minutes until golden and crispy. Serve warm!

Simple Sushi Rolls

Ingredients:

- 2 cups sushi rice
- 2 1/2 cups water
- 1/4 cup rice vinegar
- 1 tbsp sugar
- 1/2 tsp salt
- Nori sheets
- Fillings: cucumber, avocado, crab sticks, or your choice

Instructions:

1. **Cook Rice:** Rinse sushi rice under cold water until the water runs clear. Combine rice and water in a pot and cook according to package instructions.
2. **Season Rice:** In a small bowl, mix rice vinegar, sugar, and salt until dissolved. Stir into the cooked rice and let cool.
3. **Prepare Nori:** Lay a nori sheet on a bamboo mat or clean surface. Spread a thin layer of rice over the nori, leaving an inch at the top.
4. **Add Fillings:** Place desired fillings in a line across the center of the rice.
5. **Roll:** Roll the sushi tightly away from you, using the mat to help. Seal the edge with a bit of water.
6. **Slice and Serve:** Cut into bite-sized pieces and serve with soy sauce.

Enjoy making and sharing these delicious recipes!

Egg Salad Sandwiches

Ingredients:

- 6 hard-boiled eggs, chopped
- 1/4 cup mayonnaise
- 1 tsp Dijon mustard
- Salt and pepper to taste
- 1/4 cup celery, diced (optional)
- 1/4 cup green onions, sliced (optional)
- Bread or wraps for serving

Instructions:

1. **Mix Ingredients:** In a bowl, combine chopped eggs, mayonnaise, mustard, salt, pepper, and any optional ingredients.
2. **Assemble Sandwiches:** Spread the egg salad on slices of bread or wraps.
3. **Serve:** Cut into halves or quarters and enjoy!

Rainbow Veggie Pizza

Ingredients:

- 1 pizza crust (store-bought or homemade)
- 1/2 cup pizza sauce
- 1 cup shredded mozzarella cheese
- Assorted veggies: bell peppers, cherry tomatoes, spinach, purple cabbage, olives

Instructions:

1. **Preheat Oven:** Preheat the oven according to pizza crust instructions.
2. **Spread Sauce:** Spread pizza sauce evenly over the crust.
3. **Add Cheese:** Sprinkle shredded mozzarella cheese on top.
4. **Arrange Veggies:** Create a rainbow with the assorted veggies on top of the cheese.
5. **Bake:** Bake according to crust instructions until golden and cheese is bubbly. Slice and serve!

Mac and Cheese Cups

Ingredients:

- 1 cup macaroni
- 1 cup shredded cheese (cheddar or your choice)
- 1/2 cup milk
- 1 egg
- 1/4 cup breadcrumbs
- Salt and pepper to taste

Instructions:

1. **Preheat Oven:** Preheat the oven to 350°F (175°C) and grease a muffin tin.
2. **Cook Macaroni:** Cook macaroni according to package instructions; drain and let cool slightly.
3. **Mix Ingredients:** In a bowl, combine cooked macaroni, cheese, milk, egg, salt, and pepper.
4. **Fill Muffin Tin:** Divide the mixture among the muffin cups and sprinkle breadcrumbs on top.
5. **Bake:** Bake for 20-25 minutes until golden and set. Let cool slightly before serving.

Oatmeal Cookies

Ingredients:

- 1 cup butter, softened
- 1 cup brown sugar
- 1/2 cup granulated sugar
- 2 eggs
- 1 tsp vanilla extract
- 1 1/2 cups all-purpose flour
- 1 tsp baking soda
- 1/2 tsp salt
- 3 cups rolled oats
- 1 cup raisins or chocolate chips (optional)

Instructions:

1. **Preheat Oven:** Preheat the oven to 350°F (175°C) and line a baking sheet with parchment paper.
2. **Cream Butter and Sugars:** In a large bowl, cream together butter, brown sugar, and granulated sugar until light and fluffy.
3. **Add Eggs and Vanilla:** Beat in eggs one at a time, then stir in vanilla.
4. **Mix Dry Ingredients:** In another bowl, whisk together flour, baking soda, and salt. Gradually add to the butter mixture.
5. **Stir in Oats:** Fold in oats and raisins or chocolate chips if using.
6. **Drop Cookies:** Drop rounded tablespoons of dough onto the baking sheet.
7. **Bake:** Bake for 10-12 minutes until golden. Let cool on a wire rack.

Fruit Smoothie Pops

Ingredients:

- 2 cups yogurt (any flavor)
- 2 cups mixed fruit (berries, bananas, peaches)
- Optional: honey or maple syrup for sweetness

Instructions:

1. **Blend Ingredients:** In a blender, combine yogurt and mixed fruit. Add honey or syrup if desired.
2. **Pour into Molds:** Pour the mixture into popsicle molds, leaving a little space at the top for expansion.
3. **Insert Sticks:** Place sticks in the molds and freeze for at least 4 hours until solid.
4. **Serve:** Run warm water over the outside of the molds to help release the pops and enjoy!

Enjoy making these delicious recipes!

www.ingramcontent.com/pod-product-compliance
Lightning Source LLC
LaVergne TN
LVHW081326060526
838201LV00055B/2485